PIANO
VOCAL
GUITAR

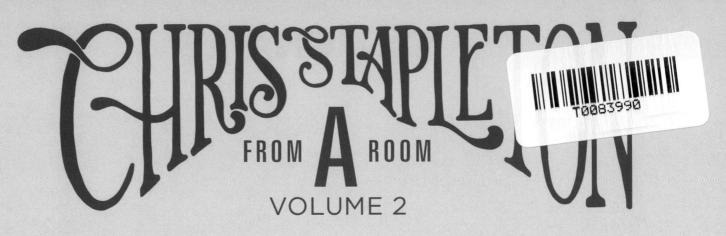

CHRIS STAPLETON
FROM A ROOM
VOLUME 2

ISBN 978-1-5400-2029-1

7777 W. BLUEMOUND RD. P.O. BOX 13819 MILWAUKEE, WI 53213

Visit Hal Leonard Online at
www.halleonard.com

MILLIONAIRE

Words and Music by
KEVIN WELCH

gold. _____
gold. _____

It can't be bought, no,
It can't be bought, no,

nev - er could be sold. _____
and it can't be sold. _____

I got
I got

love _____
love _____

e - nough to share. _____
e - nough to spare. _____

That __ makes me

a mil - lion - aire. _____

To Coda ⊕

D.S. al Coda

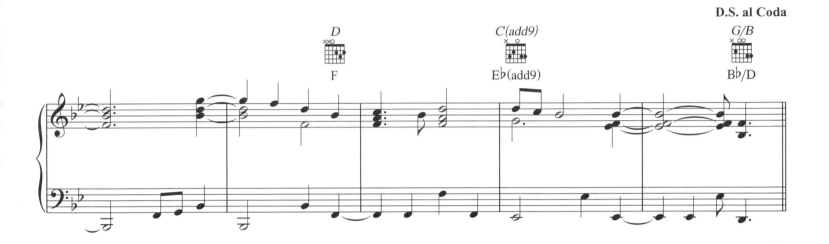

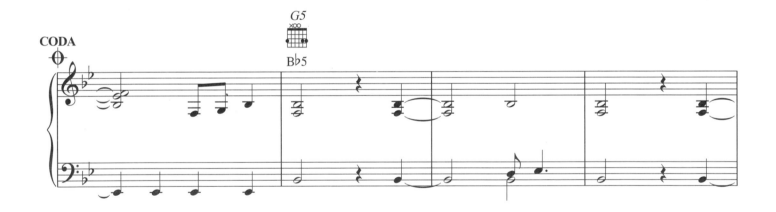

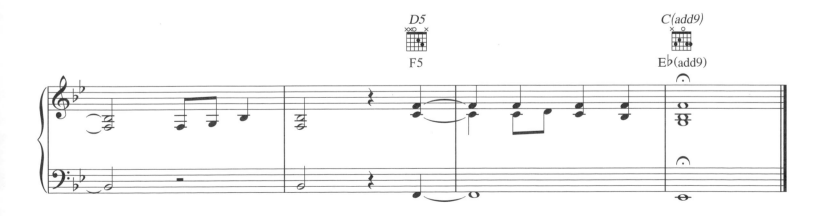

HARD LIVIN'

Words and Music by CHRIS STAPLETON
and KENDELL MARVEL

Country two-beat

I used to love to look for a fight. ___
looked a lot, but I've nev-er found ___

___ I'd ___ get drunk and shoot out the lights. ___
___ a wom-an that could set-tle me down. ___

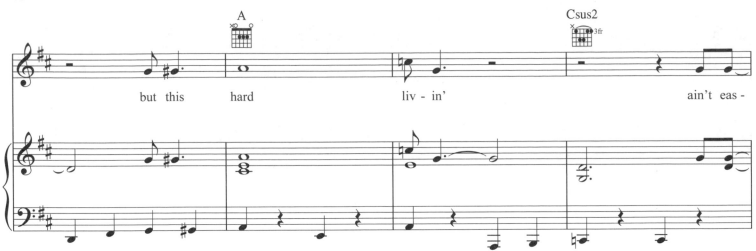

but this hard liv - in' ain't eas -

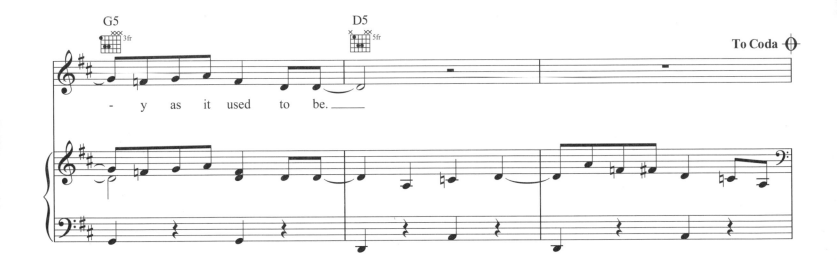

- y as it used to be. _____

To Coda ⊕

I

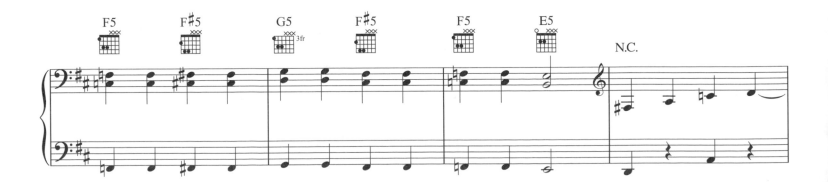

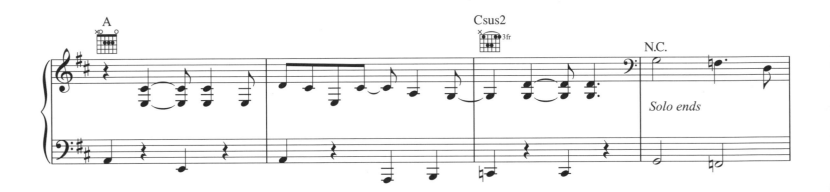

SCARECROW IN THE GARDEN

Words and Music by CHRIS STAPLETON,
WILLIAM BRICE LONG and MATT FLEENER

Moderately fast

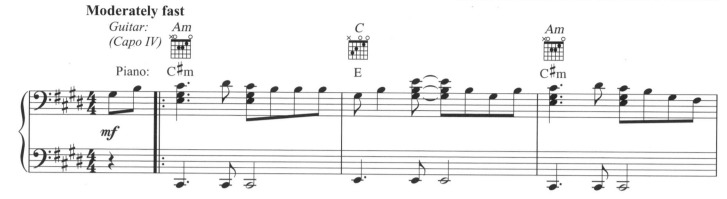

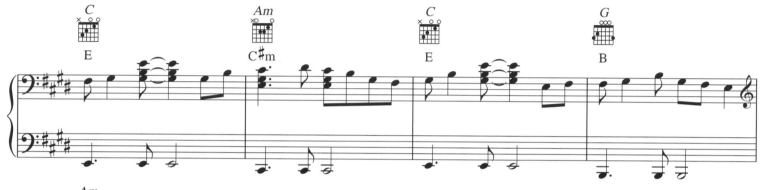

Well, he came from North - ern
Well the red - head son got

Ire - land, search - in' for the free man's ground. _ And he
old - er and took a brown-eyed wife. ___ And the

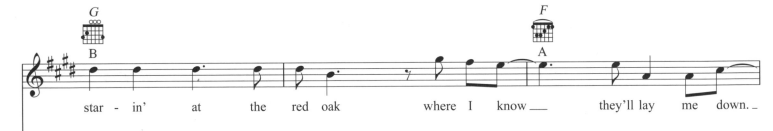

rains just seem to flood. __ And I've been think - in' 'bout __ that

riv - er, won-d'rin' how it turns __ to blood. __ I've been

sit - tin' here all morn-in'. I was sit - tin' here all night. __ There's a

Bi - ble in my left hand and a pis - tol in __ my right. __

NOBODY'S LONELY TONIGHT

Words and Music by CHRIS STAPLETON
and MIKE HENDERSON

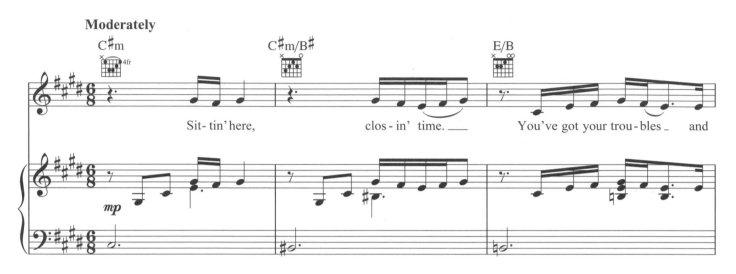

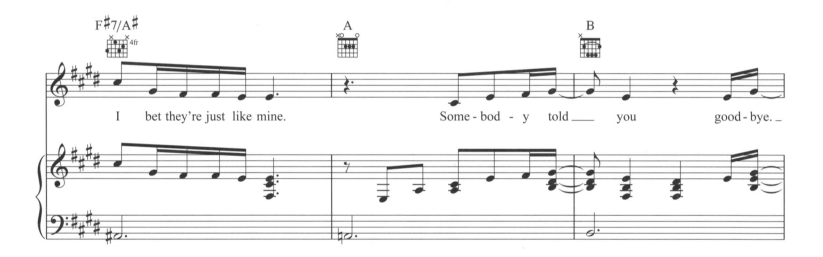

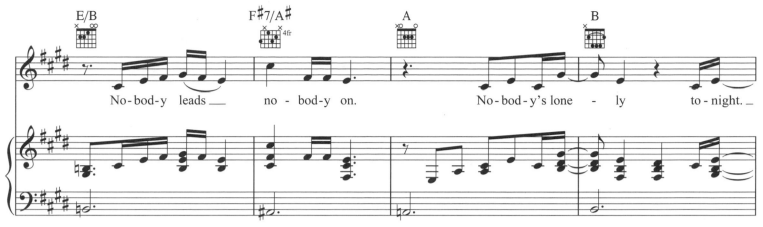

No-bod-y leads ___ no-bod-y on. No-bod-y's lone - ly to-night. ___

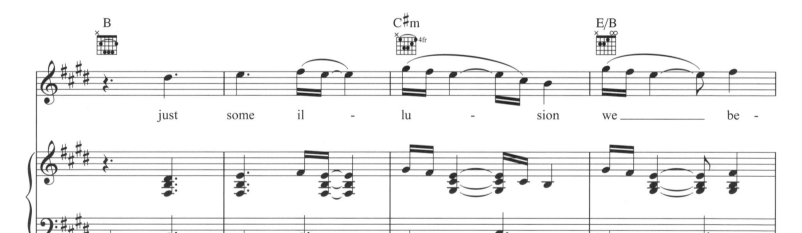

___ What's love but ___

just some il - lu - sion we ___ be -

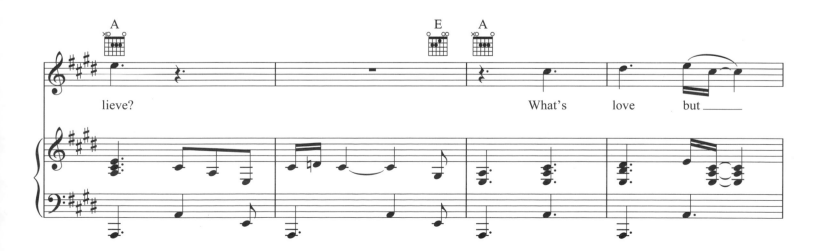

lieve? What's love but ___

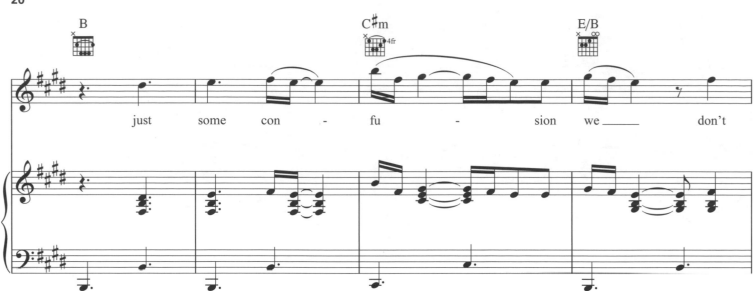

just some con - fu - sion we _____ don't

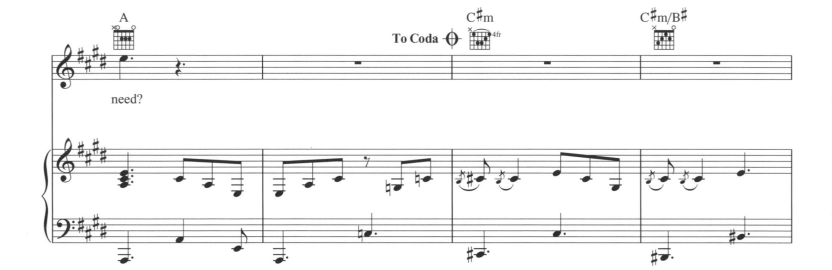

need?

To Coda ⊕

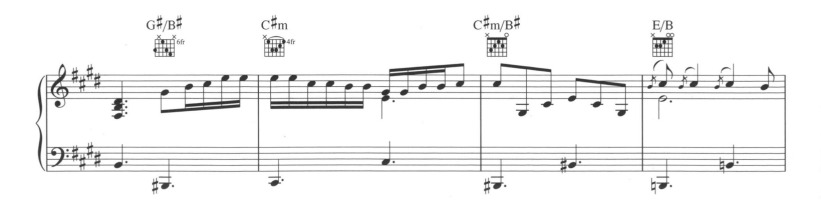

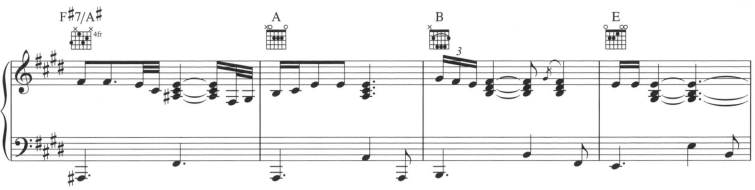

D.S. al Coda

CODA

You'll be her ___ and I'll be him __

and for a while we'll ___ pre-tend no-bod-y's lone - ly to-night.

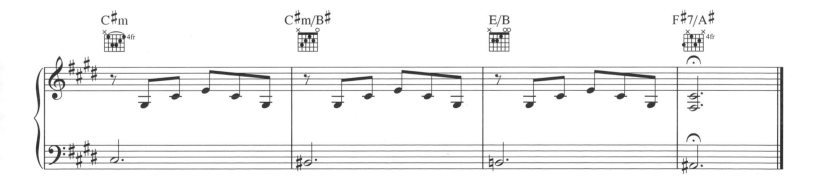

TRYIN' TO UNTANGLE MY MIND

Words and Music by CHRIS STAPLETON,
KENDELL MARVEL and JARON BOYER

Well, I drank ___ a lot of whis-key in my time. ___

Guitar solo ad lib.

And I've held ___ a lot of wom-en that were fine. ___ And I've

made a lit - tle mon - ey. _____ I blew ev - 'ry dime _

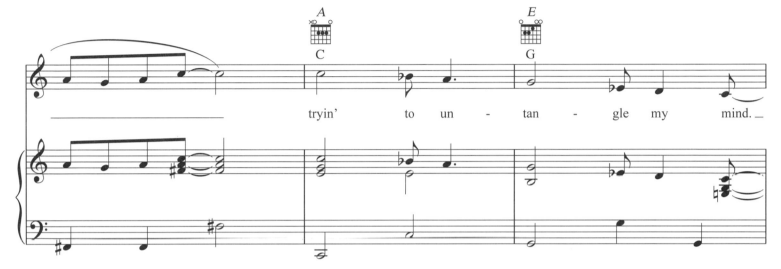

_____ tryin' to un - tan - gle my mind. _

Well, I've made _____ a lot of

Solo ends Well, I do what I _____ do _

choic - es that were wrong. _____ Let a

_____ and I don't know _____ why. _____ But I

Yes, I'm try - in' to un - tan - gle my mind. _

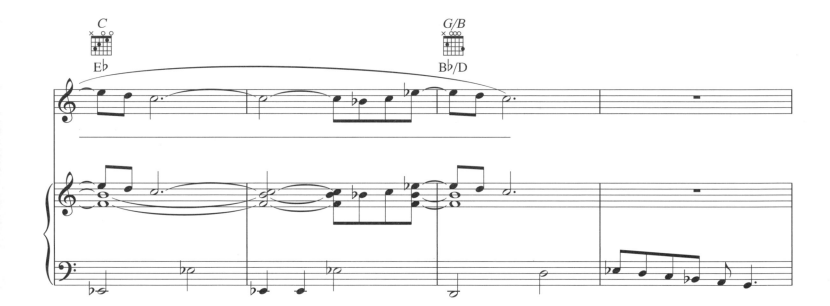

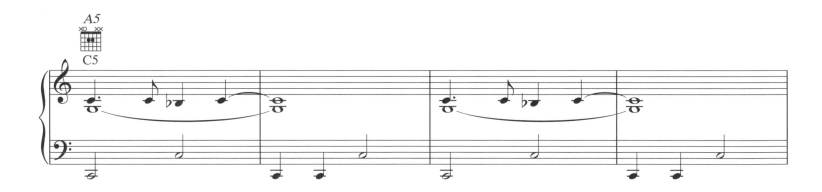

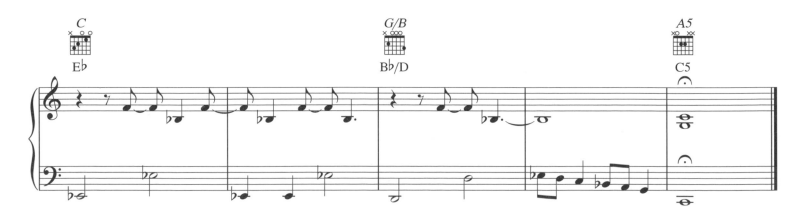

A SIMPLE SONG

Words and Music by CHRIS STAPLETON
and DARRELL HAYES

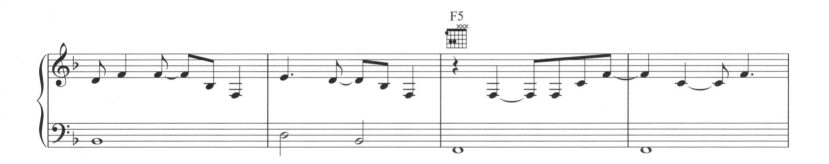

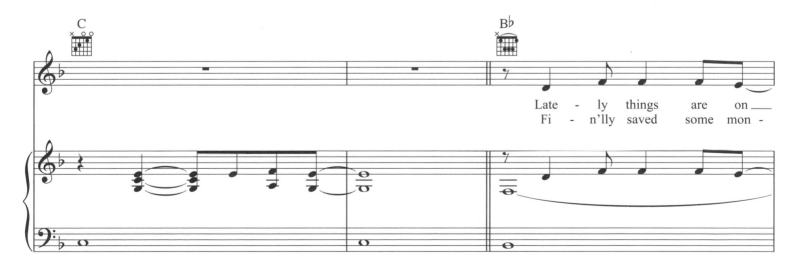

Late - ly things are on ___
Fi - n'lly saved some mon -

Call my ma - ma like I should. __
Try'n' to quit these cig - ar - ettes. __

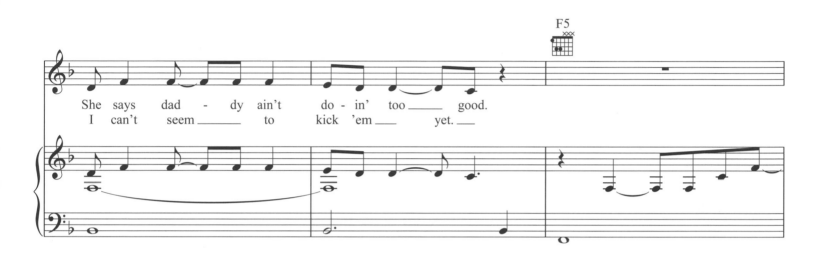

She says dad - dy ain't do - in' too ___ good.
I can't seem ___ to kick 'em ___ yet. __

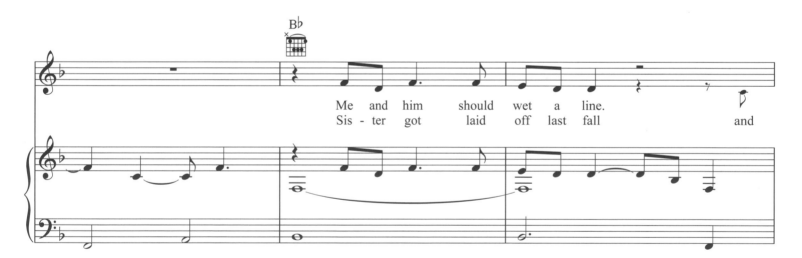

Me and him should wet a line.
Sis - ter got laid off last fall and

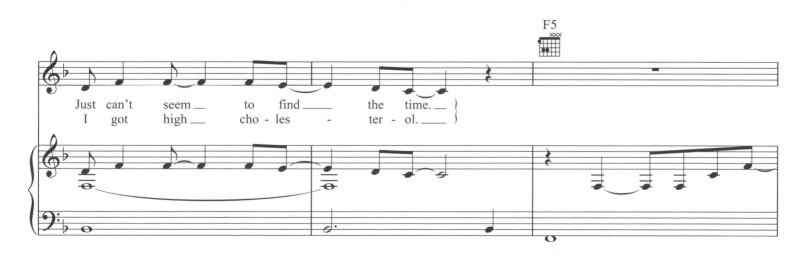

Just can't seem __ to find ___ the time. __
I got high __ cho - les - ter - ol. __

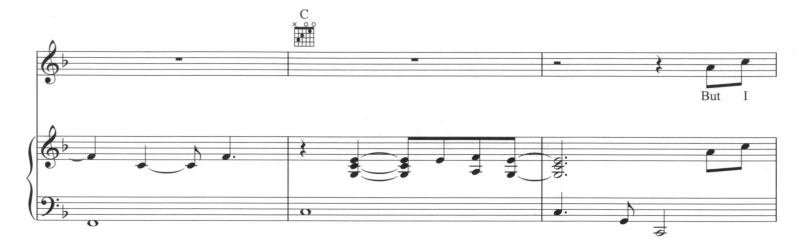

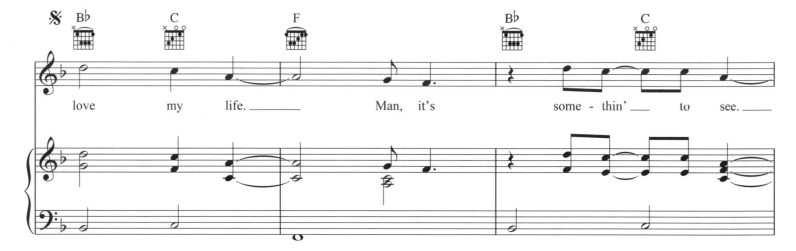

love my life._____ Man, it's some-thin'__ to see._____

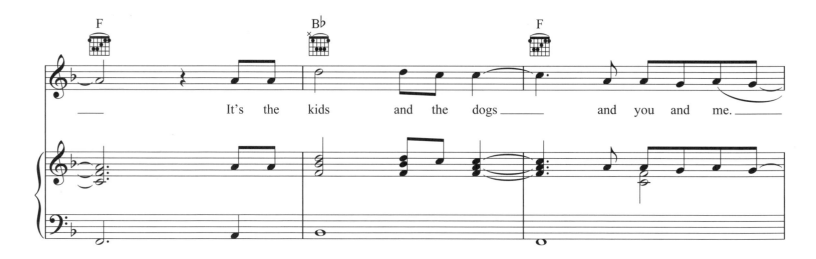

____ It's the kids and the dogs_____ and you and me._____

____ It's the way it's al - right____

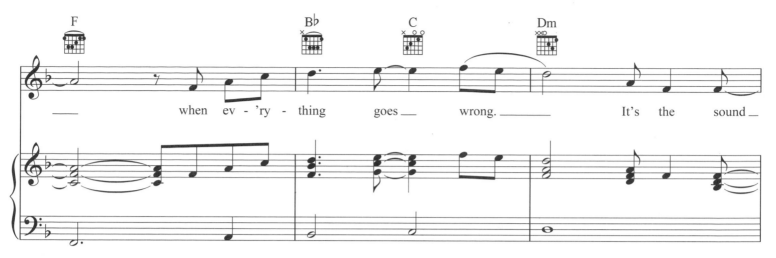

when ev - 'ry - thing goes ___ wrong. ___ It's the sound ___

___ of a slow, ___ sim - ple song. ___ sim - ple song. ___

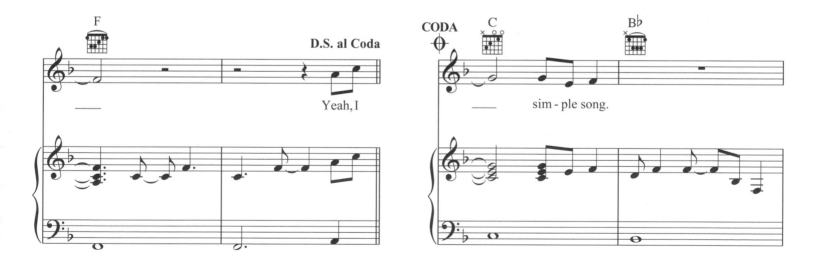

D.S. al Coda

Yeah, I ___ sim - ple song.

CODA

MIDNIGHT TRAIN TO MEMPHIS

Words and Music by CHRIS STAPLETON
and MIKE HENDERSON

Moderately

Well, ___

judge looked down, gave me for-ty days ___
whis-tle blows when the sun comes up. ___
Ten for the ju-ry and ten for the judge.

in-

stead of the fine that I could not pay.
Head to ___ floor, keep your big mouth shut.
Twen-ty more ___ to for-get my grudge.

Said, "Walk right, you'll soon be home. ___
Eat your break-fast on the ground. ___
When I get to thir-ty-nine, ___

that's the

Cross the line, ___ you'll be on your own." ___
Work like hell ___ till the sun goes down. ___
long-est day ___ in a pris'ner's mind. ___

For-ty days ___

D5

___ of shot-guns ___ and barbed ___ wire

N.C.

fenc-es.

For-ty nights ___

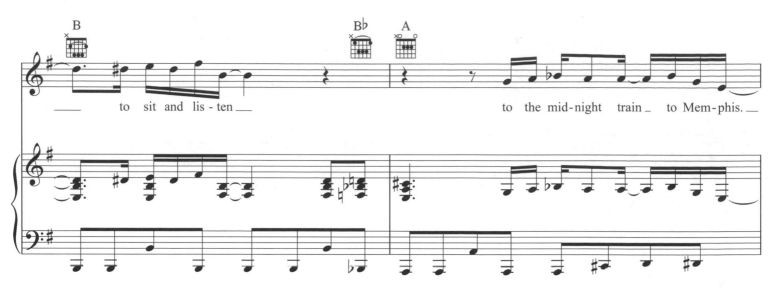

to sit and lis - ten ___ to the mid-night train ___ to Mem-phis. ___

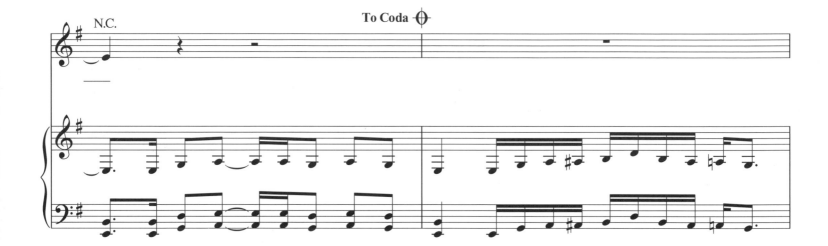

To Coda ⊕

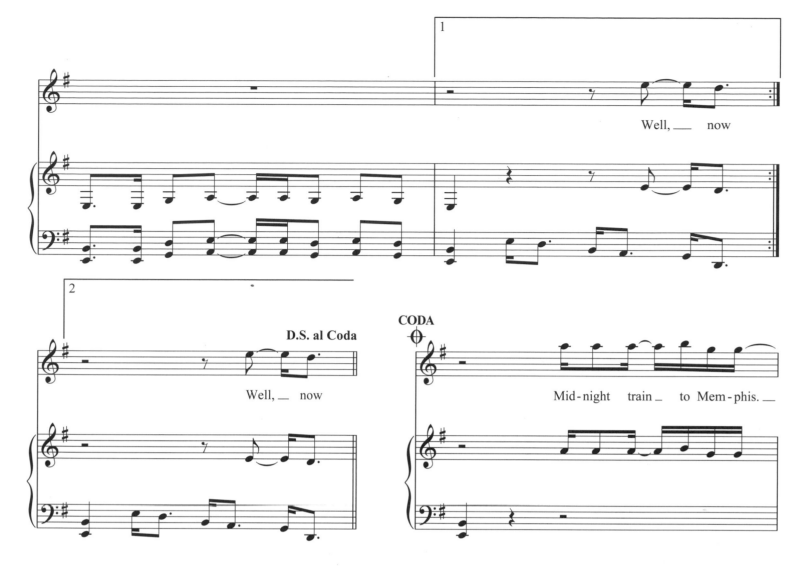

Well, ___ now

D.S. al Coda

Well, ___ now

CODA

Mid-night train ___ to Mem-phis. ___

Mid - night train ___ to Mem-phis. ___

Oh, ___ mid-night train ___ to Mem-phis. ___

rit.

DRUNKARD'S PRAYER

Words and Music by CHRIS STAPLETON
and CRISTOPHER JAMESON CLARK

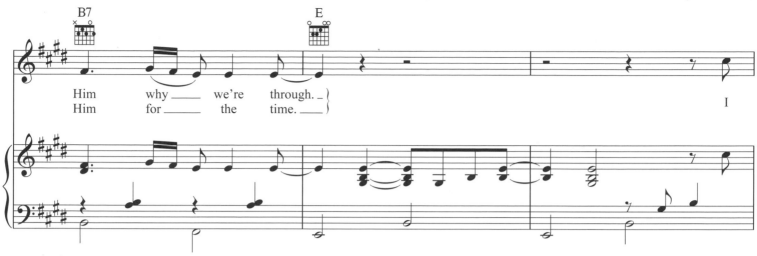

Him why ____ we're through.
Him for ____ the time. ____
I

wish that I could go to church, but I'm _____ too a-shamed _____ of me. ____

____ I hate the fact _ it takes a bot-tle _____ to

get me ____ on _____ my ____ knees. _____ And I hope _

he'll — for - give — the things — you — ain't — for - got, —

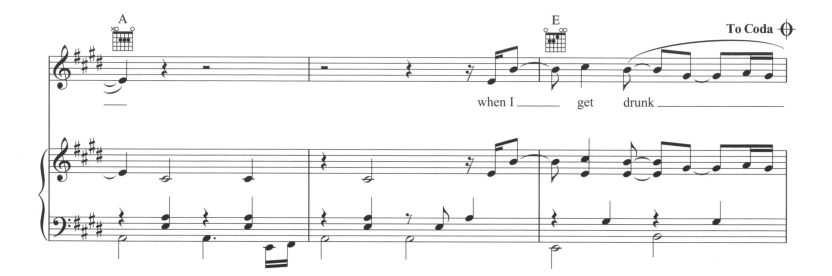

— when I — get drunk —

— and talk — to God. —

D.S. al Coda

When I __

CODA

__ and talk __ to God, __

__ oh, __ when I __

__ get drunk __ and talk __ to God. __

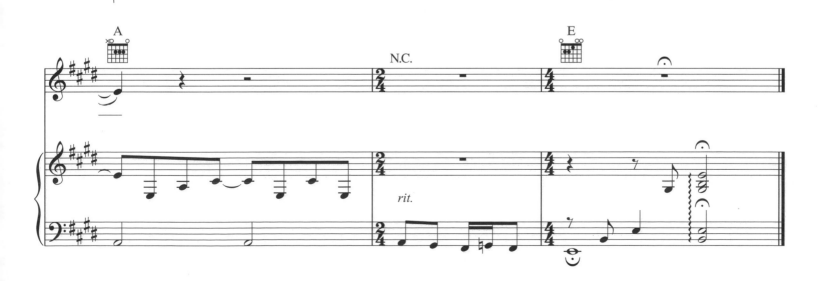

N.C.

rit.

FRIENDSHIP

Words and Music by HOMER BANKS
and LESTER A. SNELL

There are times _____ we dis - a - gree; _ we a - gree _ more _ than we
your wel - fare _____ is my con - cern. _ You weigh _ less _ than you

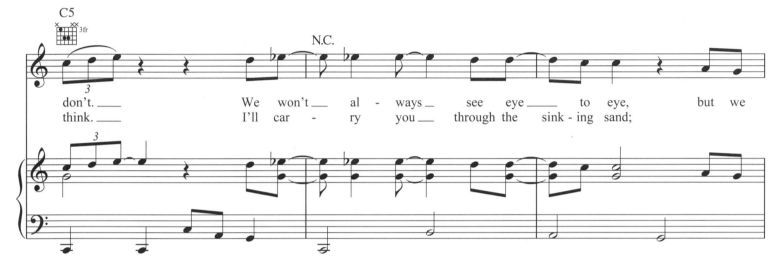

don't. ___ We won't _ al - ways _ see eye _ to eye, but we
think. ___ I'll car - ry you _ through the sink - ing sand;

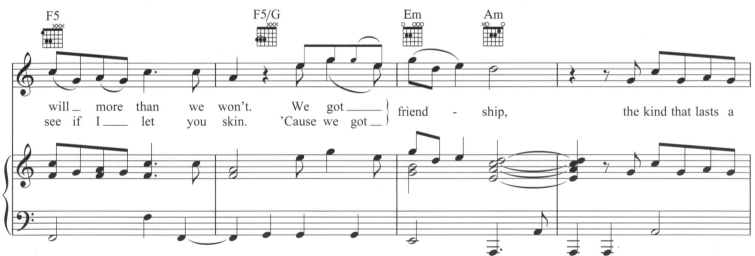

will _ more than we won't. We got _____ friend - ship, the kind that lasts a
see if I ___ let you skin. 'Cause we got _ friend - ship, the kind that lasts a

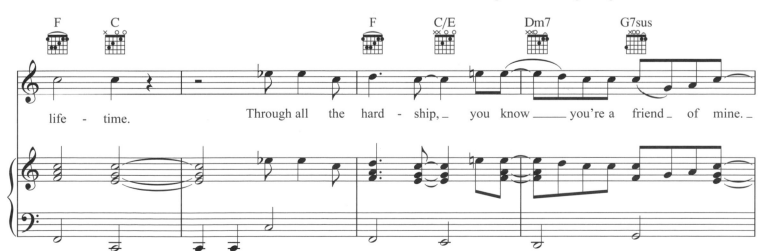

life - time. Through all the hard - ship, _ you know _____ you're a friend _ of mine. _

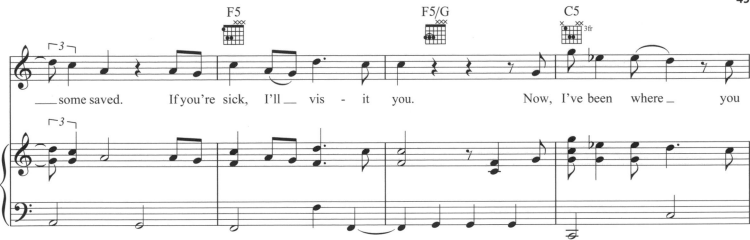

_____ some saved. If you're sick, I'll ___ vis - it you. Now, I've been where ___ you

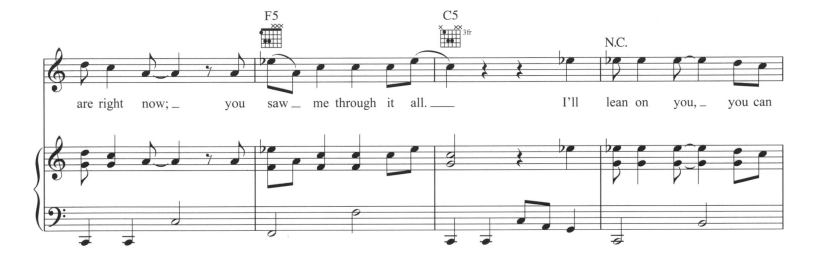

are right now; ___ you saw ___ me through it all. ___ I'll lean on you, ___ you can

lean on me. ___ I'm nev - er gon - na let you fall. 'Cause we got ___

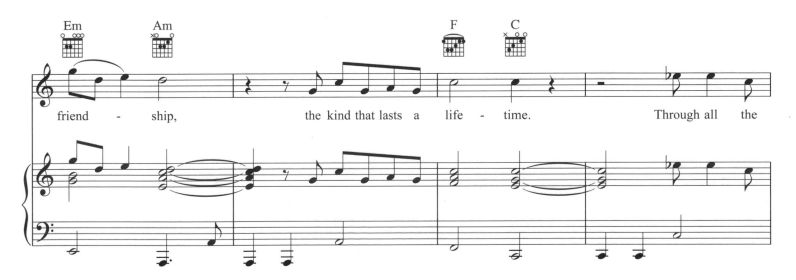

friend - ship, the kind that lasts a life - time. Through all the

hard - ship, _ you know _____ you're a friend _ of mine. _____ Yeah, we got ___

friend - ship, the kind that lasts a life - time. Through all the

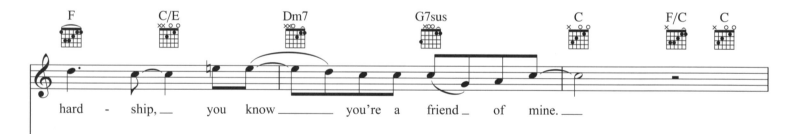

hard - ship, __ you know _____ you're a friend _ of mine. ___

Instrumental solo

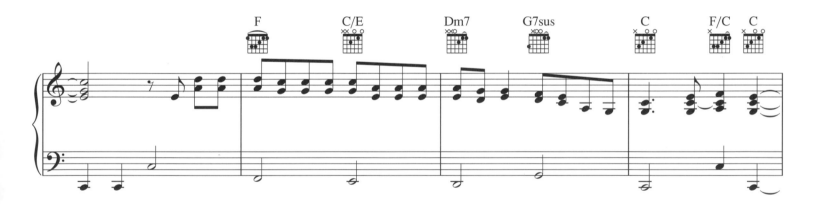

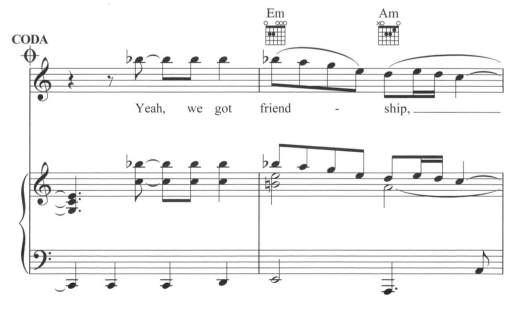

Yeah, we got friend - ship,

the kind that lasts a life - time. Through all the hard-ship,_ you know_

_____ you're a friend_ of mine._ Through_ all the hard - ship,_ you know_

_____ you're a friend_ of mine._

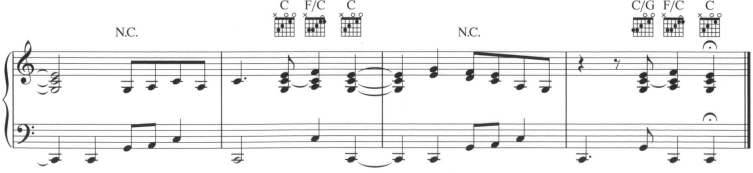